MW01228258

# Horace P. McGillicuddy

*A Little Book*
*With*
*Some Big Words*

*by*

**Larry Cloud**

This is a work of fiction. It is meant to be entertaining. The story is based upon a vivid dream I once had. The name and characteristics of the main character are products of my imagination, but in a global population of more than 8,000,000,000 people it's possible that someone resembles Horace P. McGillicuddy. There may even be someone with the same name. If so, may he please be flattered rather than offended, and perhaps be even a bit envious of my imaginary Horace's wonderful adventures.

**Larry Cloud**
**Chattanooga, Tennessee**

## Note to Readers

This little book includes some big words. Little words can express many things, but big words can express even more. Nobody really wants to go through life having only little words to use. And you can't start knowing big words too soon – but you must know what they mean, too, and always use them correctly.

That's one reason I've designed this book with quite a bit of empty space on the left-hand pages. The drawings illustrate details from the story, but they also leave plenty of room for personal notes about the big words and their meanings.

And, I've learned by experience, some people like to make their own drawings in books. There is room for that, too.

# Horace P. McGillicuddy

Do you remember, as I do, that great climactic scene in *The Music Man* movie, when the ragtag and discordant small-town boys' band, with dilapidated instruments and crummy uniforms, little talent, less training, and no experience, and a slick-looking, fast-moving, quick-thinking, and smooth-talking flimflam man for an instructor, is suddenly transformed before our very eyes into one of the finest musical organizations in the modern world – complete with **76 trombones**?

Sure, we all remember that, and we wrote it off as just another pleasant story, another tall tale, one more Hollywood movie maker's triumph, a visual trick, some pretty pictures, nothing but a lot

Welcome to
**Smithville**

Elevation 1,962 ft
Population 1,962

of smoke and mirrors. Nevertheless, we enjoyed the whole illusion; we gladly cooperated in our own deception. We called it a trick, we scoffed at the whole idea, we laughed at ourselves, and we loved every bit of it!

Yet haven't we all seen similar things in real life, things that didn't really make sense at the time, and haven't we all contributed to fooling ourselves by cooperating with the trick? Maybe we claim not to believe in magic, but still we love things that seem magical. We've done it before, and we'll happily do it again the first chance we get.

So, now, consider the strange-but-true tale of Horace P. McGillicuddy, and of *The Horace P. McGillicuddy*. Read it for yourself, then decide for yourself whether you want to believe it or not.

\*\*\*

Horace P. McGillicuddy of Smithville, California was, according to his fellow townsmen, a rather small man, quiet and thoughtful. He didn't

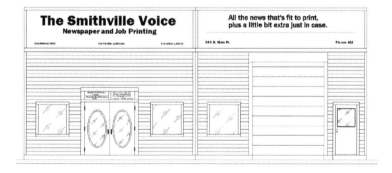

take up much room around town, and he didn't make much of a fuss, either. He was a good and honest neighbor, but not overly dynamic or gregarious – some compared him to the '*Before*' pictures in the old comic book muscle-building advertisements.

Horace worked as a printer for his hometown newspaper. He always said he loved words, loved the way words sound, one at a time or in long strings of them; he loved the way words mean things, by themselves or in combinations; he loved the way they look on paper, and figured the least he could do was to make words look their very best. Horace was responsible for getting out the thrice-weekly editions of **The Smithville Voice**, and he also hand-set the type for most of the birth, baptism, graduation, engagement, wedding, club banquet, funeral, and other formal announcements and invitations printed in Smithville for more than thirty years.

Horace and his wife Florence had only one child, their son Jeffrey, who was killed in peculiar circumstances "in the Service of his Country," as the elaborate official citation read, while he was enlisted

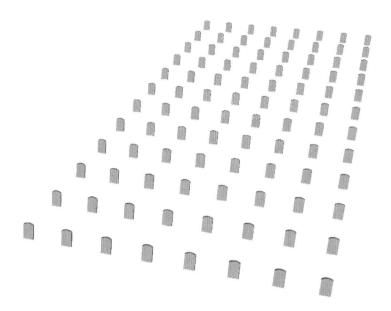

in the U.S. Army. Jeffrey's parents accepted that rather nebulous explanation and a handsome boxed medal in Jeffrey's honor, and they smiled and wept proudly during the traditional military burial service out at Smithville's scenic and quiet old Hilltop Cemetery. You know how that ceremony works: The crisp-uniformed honor guard with flags and drums, the hidden bugler playing a mournful '*Taps*,' the blank-cartridge 21-rifle salute, the whole time-honored business. It was a big day in Smithville, then the little town and its people soon got back to normal.

Florence McGillicuddy was taken ill shortly after Jeffrey's funeral, then she died peacefully a few months later. She'd lived that way, peacefully, for fifty-one years. Horace took it all in stride, it seemed, but it wasn't long before he took off his folded-paper hat, hung up his ink-stained apron, and retired from his printer's job. Said he still had some things he wanted to do in life, and guessed he'd better get on with doing them. He wasn't leaving Smithville, just quitting his job at *The Smithville*

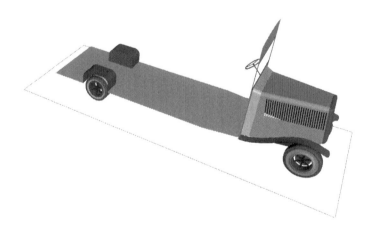

*Voice*. And he wasn't planning to loaf away the rest of his time here on Earth, either. No, Sir!

You see, years before, Horace P. McGillicuddy had bought a small old school bus, about a 1937 model. Of course, when that decrepit vehicle was originally built, *all* school buses were small. And the sturdy hill-country bus that Horace bought looked like it had been driven hard and put away wet; it was a real mess, bent and broken and rusted all over – with six flat tires. But in the ensuing years Horace had carefully and patiently rebuilt the engine, the transmission, and all the rest of the mechanical parts. He knew every bolt and nut, every bar and bearing in the whole apparatus. He said it ran like a sewing machine, purred like a kitten. Horace didn't always speak in cliches, but he always contended that people understood him when he did. Now, with the mechanical work on the old bus completed, with his family all gone, and without the obligations and hindrance of a full-time job, Horace began working in earnest on the next stage of that big personal project.

The majority of the original school bus superstructure, all rotten wood and rusted steel, had long since been removed and discarded. The strong old bus chassis, with its rugged hood, swooping front fenders, and windshield frame intact and refurbished, occupied most of the interior of a small horse-and-carriage barn on the alley behind Horace's little white home. With forty-some extra hours every week to work on the thing, Horace could now make rapid progress.

After he replaced the original two-piece windshield with a single broad expanse of clear glass and added some modern long-armed electric windshield wipers, he began to build, slowly and painstakingly, what he usually called a large rectangular parallelepiped. Then he'd laugh and explain, "You know – a big box!" And it was just that, a big box, all flat sides and square corners. Actually the roof, the top of the box, was gently curved from side to side, like the water-shedding cabin roof of a fancy boat. It was still obviously just a big box, though – tall, and narrow, and long. It

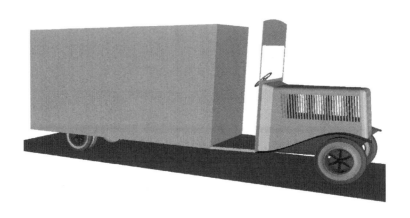

12

was a bit over 10 feet high from the ground up, not quite eight feet wide, and about 20 feet long from the windshield to the taillights. And what a box it was!

Now, Horace had never traveled very widely, but he had read extensively. He read books, and he studied maps. And he had thought extensively, which is something else, a different matter entirely. True thinking is an unusual habit for anyone in any town, small or large. He had developed certain very distinct but infrequently expressed tastes and preferences. In his rectangular parallelepiped, built atop that tough old school bus frame, Horace P. McGillicuddy had let his imagination run free. He exhibited his personal preferences and tastes, and they were eclectic tastes, indeed.

Horace liked fire trucks. He liked old-timey steam locomotives – he liked everything about a train, from cowcatcher to caboose. He liked trolley cars, and circuses and carnivals, and parade wagons and shepherd's wagons, homecoming floats and all kinds of boats, and especially those quaint old-world

gypsy wagons ... once, he had quietly but firmly declared himself to be the descendent of a fabled Romany king; with a name like McGillicuddy that was hard to substantiate, so the claim received little general acceptance. But those who were present when he said it, who saw the set of his jaw and the glint in his eye, dared not contradict him.

Anyway, Horace built, painted, and equipped a big box atop the old school bus chassis, using wood and steel and aluminum. Yes, what a box! Describing it is difficult; you just have to jump in wherever you are and start describing, because there's no obvious place to start to list all of the details, and there's certainly no obvious place to stop. No words are really adequate for the job – and no photograph or drawing ever managed to represent the contraption fully, either. (Even the drawings in this book merely indicate some generalities.)

One obvious feature was its color. Or colors. They were bright, vivid colors. Horace, though small and quiet, and generally regarded as timid, even 'mousy,' didn't like soft pastel colors. He

16

figured that red, yellow, green, and blue were good enough for God's glorious rainbow, and they were certainly good enough for Horace P. McGillicuddy. So one basic color of the machine, the front fenders, etc. of the old bus, was red. Bright red. Fire engine red. Chinese red. Whatever name for red means the reddest to you, that's the kind of red it was, over and under, around and through all the rest of it.

Then there was yellow – canary yellow, chrome yellow, sunshine yellow, whatever word for yellow says the yellowest to you, that was it! And there were greens – grass green, ivy green, pine-tree green, parrot green, and several other shades of green, but all unquestionably, undeniably, without-a-doubt *green*.

There was plenty of blue, of course: Light blue and bright blue, bold blue and cold blue, royal blue and navy blue, electric blue and neon blue, ice blue and sky blue, all of them most definitely and decidedly blue. Here and there was some purple and some orange in various shades. He used a bit of black, too, mostly in the form of fancy curlicue pin-

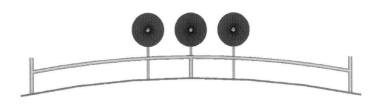

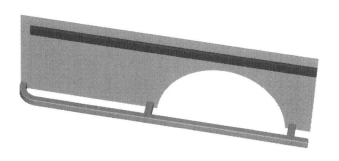

18

striping and neat thin stripes separating the various other colors, and on some of the smaller accessory parts. And what accessory parts there were!

There were brass rails – shiny tubular border rails surrounding the top of the box, convenient short handrails here and there on the vertical sides, and heavy square rails in place of running boards. Those running boards – foot rails, actually – extended from wheel to wheel of the vehicle, from the swooping front fenders to the dual chrome tailpipes. There were shiny brass horns, big as the bells of those magical movie trombones – two on each front fender, and three more atop the driver's cab. (Sorry, Horace said, only seven of them; there just wasn't enough room for 76.)

And there were lights! Myriad small running lights, regular headlights, fog lights, turn lights, brake lights, side lights, spot lights, and just plain light lights, mostly chromium plated and sparkling like everything, even in the dark.

Just for fun, he added a fancy 19th-century-locomotive-inspired smokestack right in the middle

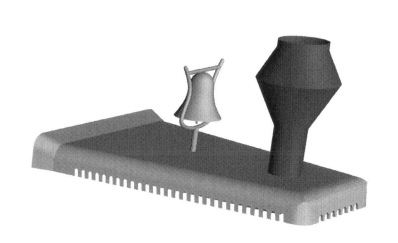

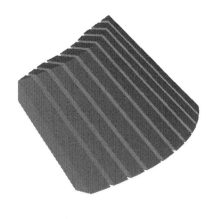

20

of the hood! Immediately behind the smokestack was a shiny brass bell on a fancy curved yoke, with a rope arranged for easy ringing. (Both the smokestack and the bell were removable for ordinary daily driving; Horace installed them only when he needed them for show, or show-off, purposes.)

The unusual front bumper was definitely utilitarian, sturdy and heavy but graceful, precisely curved and crafted of beautiful American hardwood, glowing like a piece of fine furniture. It distinctly resembled an old-fashioned locomotive cowcatcher, according to some ancients who saw it. And there was a tidy little caboose-type four-windowed cupola on top of the long tall narrow box, near the back end of the cambered roof. That rooftop cupola hid a useful air conditioner Horace had salvaged from a luxury highway bus; he planned to travel in summer, and he knew not all of America is cool.

There were eight genuine ship's portholes along the sides of the parallelepiped – all shiny brass and glass, of course. There were a couple of

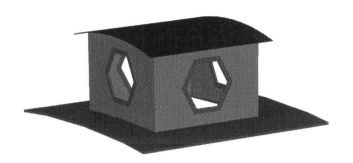

22

glorious brass ladders at the rear, leading to the gently arched top of the box. Nobody ever really needed to get on the roof, but ... well, Horace wanted brass ladders, and it was his project, so Horace had shiny yellow brass ladders. Two of them.

Several small antique stained glass windows were incorporated into the design, too, windows with circular, hexagonal, and other outline shapes, all including lots of bright and beautiful colors that sparkled in the sun. And there was a pretty bay window, or 'bow' window as Horace called it, on each long side of the box – with intricate sand-blasted designs in every pane.

Near the front center of the roof was a big transparent plastic bubble skylight – just because, Horace explained. He could glance straight up while driving, if necessary. There were flagpole sockets on both front fenders and at the four corners of the roof. Horace said those were there 'just in case' – in case he ever needed to drive the vehicle in a patriotic parade, for instance.

No one ever figured out where Horace

24

managed to get great big wide-white-sidewall tires to fit an old *school bus*, but he did. Jokingly, he said once that he got them from the Monkey Ward's mail-order catalog, but the town postman stoutly denied ever having delivered anything like those six mammoth whitewall tires. (Of course, some sly folks in town snickered that tubby old Tom the Mailman did *everything* stoutly.) Yes, even the inner tires on the rear axle were whitewalls. As a skilled printer, Horace P. McGillicuddy was a man who attended to even the least of details; if he ever did anything at all, he invariably did it right.

Horace never made any big secret about his intentions. He said he was fixing the whole thing up to live in comfortably while he did a bit of traveling, making it a rather basic but very comfortable home-on-wheels for convenience and economy. Just Horace and his dog Wolfgang would be using it, and they didn't need much to be happy. (Wolfgang was a myopic and asthmatic brown Dachshund, somewhat past his prime.)

No, no pictures have ever done justice to the

external appearance of this unique machine. But what was *inside* that wonderful big bright-colored box? No one has ever seemed to know for sure! It's not that nobody ever peeked in through the eight round portholes and the various little stained glass polygons, or opened one of the neat doors, or got invited inside for a grand tour of the premises; it's just that no one could ever remember exactly what he or she *saw* when they did get a look at it. As with the encyclopedic and kaleidoscopic exterior, the interior was utterly dazzling; it was essentially indescribable. And, again, there are no photos of it.

It's reasonable to assume that Horace installed the basic equipment for comfortable traveling and resting – things like a small gas stove and oven, a battery-powered refrigerator, a couple of small sinks and a toilet and a shower, with the necessary freshwater and used-water tanks. And, of course, a comfortable easy chair or two, a simple but sufficient bed and a doggy bed, and various interior lights. But, again, nobody could say for sure!

Some have said the bus's inside was like a

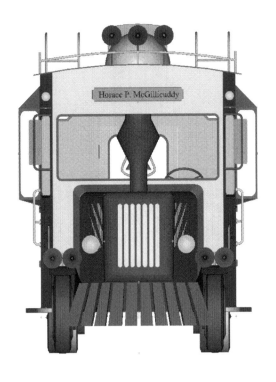

deluxe Pullman private railway coach, all carved and varnished and polished walnut wood with Persian carpets and lots of brass lamps and silver mirrors, while others likened it to a rustic old-time country general store with all of its intriguing sights and smells. Even when the occasion was fresh in local minds, there always seemed to be wide differences of opinion as to the contents of *The Horace P. McGillicuddy*. Somehow the thing made a different impression on every one who ever saw it. Everyone agreed it was wonderful; nobody agreed on the details. In that sense it was magical. And, as we will see, all that was true wherever the vehicle went.

Oh, yes, that name – the name was one of the last details Horace completed on his marvelous machine. In large but discreet script letters, in brilliant gold leaf with minuscule black borders, the name *The Horace P. McGillicuddy* was displayed on both of the front doors. (While he was modifying the old bus, Horace attached regular swinging front doors to each side of the cab – he planned it that way, he said, to have a nice 'field' to put the gold

30

leaf name on. And, besides, he chuckled, the school bus was never his favorite kind of vehicle; he had to disguise the old thing's origins some way! Hence that useful extra front door on the driver's side.) Underneath the formal and fancy gold leaf script name, it said 'Smithville, California' in simple black letters with gold highlights. It was a nice touch, his neighbors thought. And it was a perfectly adequate address, since ZIP codes hadn't been invented yet, way back then.

Above the windshield, and above the back door, were fine carved and varnished name-boards like those on fancy yachts, proclaiming this to be *The Horace P. McGillicuddy.* Horace was always sort of modest and shy, but he was never fanatical about it!

Now that those matters have been covered, the Horace P. McGillicuddy story must be placed in the proper context to give it due justice and to explain its full significance. In those days, not really all that long ago, there wasn't the profusion of factory-built camper trucks, camping trailers, mobile homes,

Horace P. McGillicuddy

motor homes, RVs, and luxury private highway cruiser buses that we see everywhere nowadays. There were a few rustic camping mobiles of one variety or another, the majority of them home-made ('handcrafted' was too good a word for most of them); relatively few were made in a factory, and then only if the owner was an affluent industrialist or entertainer. Either way, campers of any kind were rare back then.

So, yes, the Horace P. McGillicuddy big-box-on-wheels was definitely a unique vehicle when Horace built it. And it is unique today – we know it still exists, and some folks claim it is still rolling. But that's irrelevant at the moment, and it's getting ahead of our story; the thing of interest right now is what *The Horace P. McGillicuddy* is known to have been and done when it was new.

Horace eventually got his big box on wheels finished. Then he went over everything with a fine-toothed comb. Tightening, adjusting, polishing, making minor revisions and needful improvements – it all took time and thought and effort. Now, some

33

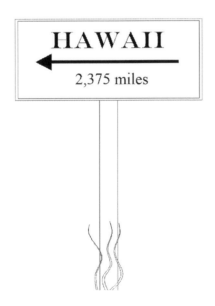

people would think that is monotonous, boring, stultifying. But not Horace; oh, no, not our Horace. Whistling, laughing, frequently rubbing his hands together and nearly dancing in satisfaction and anticipation, Horace enjoyed every bit of it. He was building a masterpiece! His dog and prospective traveling companion Wolfgang didn't really share the man's excitement, but Horace wasn't offended; he knew that was just old Wolfgang's way.

Finally it was time to prove the validity of his concept and the quality of his workmanship. Horace packed a few supplies – and Wolfgang – into his motorized version of a gypsy caravan and took a short trip west, driving casually through the hills to a small town on the coast. There were no major mechanical problems, and only a few small 'bugs' that he was able to correct as soon as they appeared.

Horace gingerly dipped the machine's front tires in the Pacific Ocean, then spent a quiet night camped under a huge oak tree. They returned home the next day by a different route, and Horace declared himself satisfied with his idea and with his

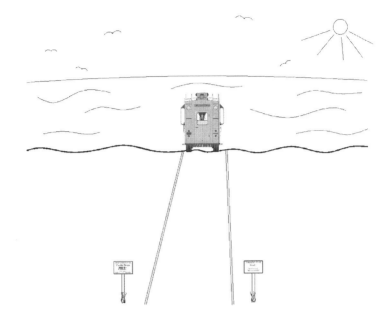

Dip your wheels in the
**Pacific Ocean**
*FREE!*
*Courtesy of*
*Smugglers Point Beach Committee*

Smugglers Point
Beach

Please help keep
California beautiful

results. He did make a few minor revisions and refinements to the interior arrangements, to improve his own comfort and Wolfgang's. Then ...

Then, at last, the big day arrived. Residents of Smithville found a small, meticulously hand-set announcement in a little box at the bottom of the front page of Tuesday's *Voice*. Horace would be leaving town early Friday morning, taking a first major exploratory trip in his recently-completed creation.

The *Voice* reporter interviewed Horace and published the results for all to read on Thursday: Horace loved Smithville and the people in it, but his 'Romany blood' must be satisfied. His longtime home would be left intact for the duration, minus only the few necessities he had already transferred into *The Horace P. McGillicuddy* for use while roaming. He and Wolfgang were simply going to hit the road for a while, to drift with the winds and the seasons – or against them, as it was convenient.

He said he'd always liked the harmonious and poetic names of American towns, and now he aimed

# Horace P. McGillicuddy to Depart Friday Morning

Horace says he and Wolfgang plan to live in his newly finished caravan and "to drift with the winds and the seasons, or against them, as convenient."

He says he will stay in touch and will return to Smithville in good time.

Godspeed, Horace!

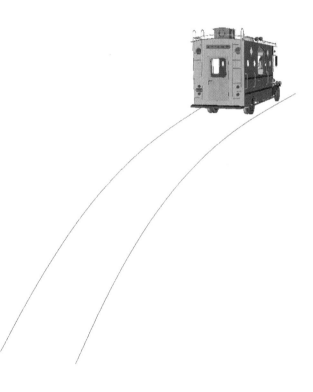

to visit some of those intriguing places for himself. *Via* highways and byways, Horace intended to see a few of the finer points of the country. It's not that he wasn't satisfied with the lovely hills and ancient forests around Smithville, mind you, but just that he had suppressed the wanderlust and the wondering all his life, and now felt entitled and obligated to cater to it for a while. They'd be hearing from him – the mails still ran six days a week. (And, to prove that this story is indeed dated, postage stamps only cost four cents, and the mails ran rapidly and reliably, too.)

And that was that! Horace P. McGillicuddy, *The Horace P. McGillicuddy*, and Wolfgang quietly left Smithville early on Friday morning as planned. The adventure had begun, and Smithville folks would be kept aware of their progress.

But, strangely, the prevailing tale of that great excursion as it is still being told is not so much the story of Horace and Wolfgang and the sights they saw, the people they met, the gentle adventures, simple pleasures, and trifling difficulties they had,

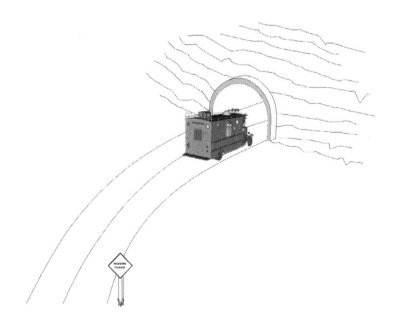

and the many new things they saw and learned in their travels 'with the winds and the seasons – or against them, as convenient.' What we know of Horace's wanderings doesn't come primarily from his frequent three-cent postcards to the folks back home; no, not at all.

No, most of the story about the travels of Horace P. McGillicuddy and *The Horace P. McGillicuddy* (the two Horaces are now generally indistinguishable in folks' minds) is actually the story of what *other* people saw *of* them, what *was seen of* The Horace P. McGillicuddy during that random and relaxed Romany roaming. A stranger story never came out of Hollywood. Or out of Washington, D.C. either, for that matter.

We can reconstruct the travels of Horace, Wolfgang, and *The Horace P. McGillicuddy*, and their impact on a great many people, by examining old postcards that were preserved by various residents of Smithville, and by reading accounts published in numerous small-town newspapers along the trail of Horace P. McGillicuddy. Come

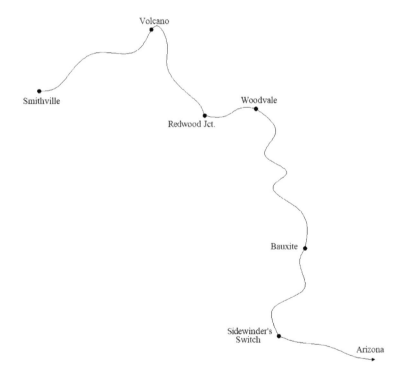

Volcano

Smithville

Woodvale

Redwood Jct.

Bauxite

Sidewinder's
Switch

Arizona

42

along now, see for yourself, and form your own opinion about all of this.

*\*\*\**

It seems that Horace and company primarily followed what most of us call 'the old roads.' Back then, some of them may actually have been *new* roads, even though they were pretty rudimentary by our modern four-lanes, limited-access, divided-highway standards. But school buses are tough by necessity, and Horace was in no hurry at all; smooth roads were not mandatory because speed was *not* of the essence. His first few days' travels were simply reported in the *Voice* as a brief, ongoing, after-the-fact itinerary:

Friday  –     Volcano, California
Saturday  –   Redwood Junction
Sunday  –     Woodvale (a short day)
Monday  –   Bauxite (a real 'low,' Horace said)
Tuesday  –    Sidewinder's Switch
Wednesday  –   Into Arizona

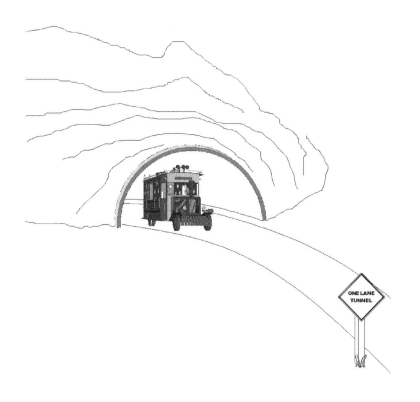

ONE LANE
TUNNEL

So it went for a couple of weeks. The *Voice* and numerous citizens of Smithville received scenic picture postcards or ordinary U.S. Postal Cards just about daily. Horace and Wolfgang were both well, were taking it easy, were seeing a great deal of new territory, and were enjoying themselves immensely. Well, Horace was, anyway. Wolfgang slept a lot, and sometimes exhibited mild symptoms of seasickness, or at least carsickness. What else would anyone expect to learn from a new and inexperienced tourist, dutifully reporting home by mail as promised, without elaboration?

But then a different sort of cards and letters began to arrive at the Smithville Post Office. These weren't as laconic as Horace's reports; most of them exhibited a certain urgency, a mild excitement, or anxious wonder. Addressed to 'Postmaster,' or 'Mayor,' 'Editor,' 'Councilman,' etc., these items contained long hand-written (or hand-printed) notes or questions, and sometimes included clippings from local newspapers. An interested observer back then could have followed Horace's route, albeit several

days belatedly, just by studying the successive postmarks on these inquiries.

Unfortunately for us, and for the more devoted and scholarly historians interested in precisely chronicling those long-past roamings, no one in those early days thought of saving and collecting and organizing all of these comments on the wanderings of Horace P. McGillicuddy and *The Horace P. McGillicuddy.*

What a treasure has been lost! But the letters that still exist are a revelation in themselves. A few excerpts are presented here, in roughly chronological and, therefore, geographical order:

** *Postmark – Pecos, Arizona:*

"Who is Horace P. McGillicuddy, of Smithville, California? A gaudily decorated old truck of some sort passed through Pecos early this morning and created quite a stir. Not just because it was the only 'foreign' vehicle to go through town all forenoon, but because it was such a truly outlandish affair. All three of the downtown loafers' dogs

Welcome to
**Three Creeks**

Max **30** Speed

Proud home of
**Sgt. Fred Jackson**

chased the thing from the town square plumb out to the east city limits, and returned looking kind of foolish but also somewhat thoughtful. Buddy Tompkins, commonly known as our village idiot, tried to hitch a ride on the vehicle, but is way too chubby and lazy to run that fast, so he wasn't able to catch up. Please reply, so we can tell the rest of the populace what it was we saw!"

** *Postmark – Three Creeks, Arizona:*

"Shortly after noon, residents of Three Creeks, Arizona were startled to observe the passing of a garishly-painted omnibus moving eastward along the highway through our town. Reports vary as to the details of this vehicle, but several observers agreed on at least one thing: Sgt. Fred Jackson, honored veteran of the Great World War, now 73 years old, portly, and usually found dozing in an old rocking chair, was seen strutting *in full doughboy uniform with ribbons, medals, and an ancient rifle*, directly in front of the strange truck or whatever it was. Six beautiful American flags graced the

Welcome to
**Aguas Piedras**

We Move Slowly, so --
Please Drive Slowly!

vehicle, John Philip Sousa marches were being played on an invisible loudspeaker system, and several people reported that thousands of firecrackers and other fireworks were being shot off as the little parade passed through town. Can you give us any details as to the person, Horace P. McGillicuddy, whose name was written on the sides of this apparition, and what he is up to?"


** *Postmark – Aguas Piedras, New Mexico:*

"We are a small town on the edge of an isolated old desert reservation. We don't have a fire department; adobe doesn't burn very well, and there's not much else around here that will burn, either. The relentless sun roasted everything out long ago! Most of us are elderly and tired, poorly educated folks who live simply, and we're certainly not noted for being highly imaginative or excitable. But several people have declared emphatically that yesterday afternoon, in the middle of *siesta*, a shiny bright red *fire truck* sped down the middle of our

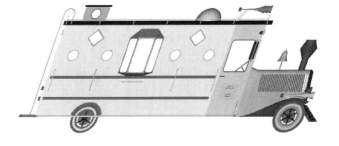

52

one dusty street. Three small boys are known to have received scoldings, or worse, for 'lying' to their mothers about it. One old gentleman who never does much but sleep and is not known to have spoken aloud for at least a decade, now talks almost nonstop – but he really isn't sure about what he thinks he might have seen during a brief waking fit. If Horace P. McGillicuddy really is from your city, please tell us something about him!"

** *Postmark – Ingleville, Colorado:*

"*NEWS BRIEF*: A strange sight thrilled numerous citizens of Ingleville this morning. About 10:15, it is reported, a rainbow-colored 'caravan' bearing the legend *'Horace P. McGillicuddy, Smithville, California'* on its doors began a stately procession down our main street. Estimates of the speed of the vehicle vary, from barely two miles per hour to somewhat over the posted speed limit. Some observers report hearing a siren, others heard bells, and still others thought it sounded like a steam calliope playing – but of those, none could affirm

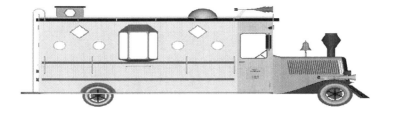

54

that they have ever actually heard a genuine steam calliope.  Dogs did howl by the dozens, and many children somehow managed to appear on the sidewalks – waving small American flags! – in spite of it being during school hours.  Four gentlemen watching in front of Godby's Hardware said they saw three crazy-garbed circus clowns scampering all around, upon, over and under this automotive phenomenon, and Mr. Charles Wilson, the honorable mayor of Ingleville, affirms that the vehicle was an accurate reproduction of a Ringling Brothers circus wagon that he saw in the East back in 1927.  Your editor is presently attempting to contact the newspaper publisher in Smithville, California, to establish particulars on this Horace P. McGillicuddy, if possible."

** *Postmark – Nelson, Kansas:*

"Could you please tell us something about Horace P. McGillicuddy, whoever or whatever he is, of Smithville?  A vehicle passed through here on U.S. 50 this evening, and was described by several

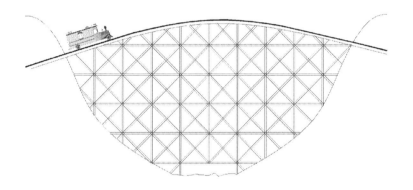

respected adults as looking just like an old 4-4-0 *American* steam locomotive, with tender and caboose. As a concerned citizen, and as a dedicated steam-train enthusiast, I would like to confirm these reports. I was cooling off in my bathtub at the time, but I did distinctly hear the sound of a steam whistle, and thought I was dreaming. First, we are over four miles from the only surviving railroad track around here, and second, any train whistles that we might hear now, under any circumstances, are the horns of Diesel locomotives. Please – tell me what you can about Horace P. McGillicuddy, and I will publish the details for the edification of our people."

***

And so it goes. Notes, letters, cards, clippings – but never any photos! – from Nebraska, from Iowa, from Missouri, Illinois and Kentucky. Several from Indiana and Ohio, some from Pennsylvania, and a very few from scattered points further east. Oh, it's certain that Horace went as far east as he

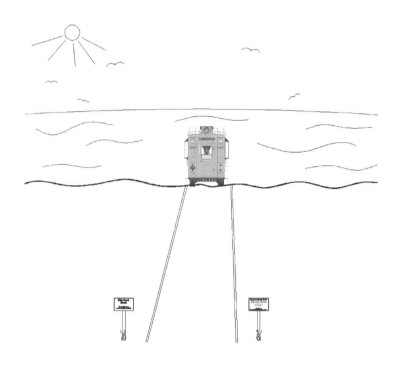

**Kitty Hawk Beach**

Please help keep
North Carolina beautiful

Dip your wheels in the
**Atlantic Ocean**
*FREE!*

*Courtesy of
The Kitty Hawk Beach Committee*

could go, all the way to the coast, even symbolically dipping his tires in the Atlantic Ocean. And he went to several different historic spots up and down that eastern coast, in fact. But it has been surmised that the learned (or dazed) hordes in the vicinity of New York and Washington, etc. aren't as easily amazed or amused by strange sights as are the rest of the true and honest American population. The evidence is that Easterners are so thoroughly and continually surrounded by outlandish things that one more oddity doesn't really grab their attention.

Horace's return trip to Smithville, by what could loosely be called the Southern route, produced an increasing number of queries to the authorities in Smithville as he proceeded westward. Some letters mentioned gilded carriages with dazzling white (or glossy black) horses wearing silver harnesses and head plumes, several were certain that a venerable steamboat had whistled and paddle-wheeled its way along a quiet, oak-shaded antebellum Main Street, and one imaginative soul described an apparent re-enactment of a black-smoke-pouring steamboat

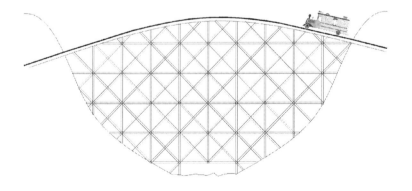

60

*race*! But that incident is generally considered to be apocryphal, and is discounted by the true scholars who diligently concern themselves with the genuine McGillicuddy history.

Anyway, Horace, *The Horace*, and Wolfgang eventually got back home safe and sound. Horace once said that, like Grand Ole Opry singer Hank Snow had recently claimed, "I've been everywhere, Man! – and a lot of other places, too." *The Horace* was just as shiny, just as sound, and just as remarkable as when the journey started; it seems the citizens of Smithville really did recognize its uniqueness after all, although they didn't quite get the same effect that others had received from it. Various old but true proverbs probably explain the general attitude in Horace's own home town; they knew him well, perhaps too well, and didn't appreciate him the way they should have.

Horace willingly gave a few simple speeches about his adventure. Particularly well-received was his talk, repeated at every church in Smithville and elsewhere for miles around, about his various

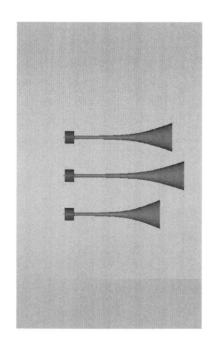

'Biblical' side trips. Horace said that several times he deliberately deviated from the obvious main route in order to visit such obscure towns as Bethel and Bethlehem, Jerusalem, Ephesus, Smyrna, Thyatira, Sardis, and Philadelphia, Cairo and Rome and Athens, Bagdad and Caesarea and Damascus. He knew he'd never manage to make a tour of the real Holy Land on the far eastern end of the Mediterranean Sea, so he figured the least he could do was to visit those American namesakes. He always sounded humble and almost apologetic whenever he said that he'd even been to see Alpha and Omega, too.

In spite of Horace's original plans for more such trips to more such sites, he never managed to take another tour nearly so extensive as that first one. Oh, there were some short, three-to-five-day relatively local drives, and several special appearances in various nearby holiday parades, but for reasons of his own Horace once turned down an urgent invitation to drive in the Rose Parade. All he said was that crowds made him nervous, and it

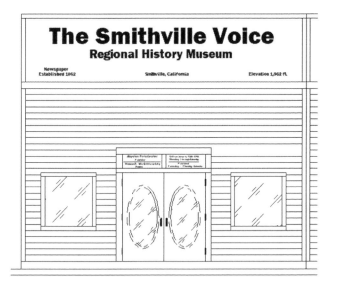

wasn't as much fun any more, what with Wolfgang gone, and all.

And now, today, several decades later, Horace is gone, too; has been for several years. His remains rest beside Florence and Jeffrey, out at Hilltop. Their neat old white home is owned by a nice young couple with two pretty little yellow-haired daughters who regularly put fresh flowers on Wolfgang's grave in the far back corner of the yard.

As with hundreds of other once famous, respected, and quite useful local newspapers, *The Smithville Voice* is defunct. In his will, the publisher left the aging wooden downtown building to the town, with a significant cash endowment and the provision that it be used for a regional history museum. There wasn't much progress in that direction for a few years, but finally a new mayor began to make things happen.

And you might guess what the largest, most famous, and most popular exhibit in that tidy downtown storefront museum is ...

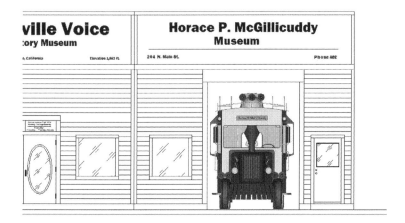

**ville Voice**
**:ory Museum**

:, California                    Elevation 2,962 ft.

# Horace P. McGillicuddy
## Museum

204 N. Main St.                                    Phone 402

*The Horace P. McGillicuddy* has been preserved as a tourist attraction for everyone to see and enjoy. The older boys of the town keep the now-venerated vehicle clean and polished, with the senior men's critical supervision, and high school auto shop students keep it tuned up and running like a sewing machine, purring like a kitten. Oh, for a couple of weeks late each year the little museum hangs out a *Closed For Maintenance* sign, but otherwise you can stop in and look around just about any time, if you're ever in Smithville. It's free, and nearly everyone who visits agrees it's worth the time and effort.

By now the story of Horace and his customized old bus and their convoluted travels has become something of a legend, and Smithville has become a serious destination for those who call themselves 'the true believers.' And the legend isn't confined to Smithville, California, either.

No, it isn't. If you follow the minor blue highways or the thin red lines on the old maps, if you can discern the winding old gray routes on

68

modern road maps, if you will get off the busy Interstates and avoid the new four-lane bypasses, if you take the time to go through some of the county-seat and country farm towns and even abandoned ghost towns, if you wind along beside the broad, slow old rivers, take the designated scenic routes, and so forth, you just may catch up with Horace P. McGillicuddy.

At least, you won't be too far behind him. Stop at a country crossroads store on a cool, bright summer morning; rest awhile in a courthouse-square diner during a hot noon hour; visit a little old barber shop or a shadowy pool hall an hour or so before supper time. Maybe a country church is having Sunday afternoon dinner-on-the-grounds; don't miss that! Be friendly, not snooty or snoopy, buy yourself and someone else a Coke or an ice cream bar, perhaps just casually mention something strange that you've seen or heard of in *your* home town, and then wait a while. Give folks time to get used to you, and give them time to think. Remember, most people say they don't believe in magic, but we've all

69

seen some things that seemed to be magical. We love such things, and we never forget them ... never.

Before long somebody will begin to tell about seeing, or of hearing about someone who saw, or of knowing someone who knew somebody who thought he saw, something really strange right there in that very town, or maybe the next town down the road. Perhaps the thing that was seen looked like a fire truck, or a circus wagon, or a steam locomotive, or even a Mark Twain riverboat. Memories may be getting hazy, but of one thing you can be certain: In the case of memories that involve *The Horace P. McGillicuddy*, the truth as those good folks once knew it has not been embellished by one *iota*. If anything, the memories are but mild approximations to the 'truth,' mere faded and watered-down versions that fall far short of the vivid impressions those local citizens had on that wonderful day when Horace P. McGillicuddy passed their way.

And, whether you choose to believe it or not, some will try to convince you that the *thing*, whatever it is – and it has apparently been a lot of

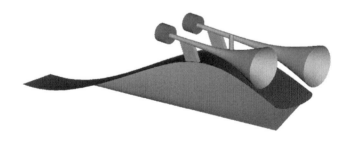

different things to a lot of different people in a lot of different places at a lot of different times – the contraption is still roaming the country. *The Horace P. McGillicuddy* is alive!

Even now, nearly a lifetime after that first momentous journey, reports and queries still arrive at little old Smithville, California from places like Ada and Adin, from Ames and Amity, Amo and Amos, Arab and Aroma, Avilla and Manila, Bald Knob and Bug, Bee Ridge and Pea Ridge and Persimmon Ridge, Beanblossom and Bell Buckle and Beulah Heights, Brisco and Cisco, Cabot and Cabool, Chickamauga and Churubusco, Chili and Chillicothe, Damariscotta and Dover and Durbin, Decoy and Deming, Eden and Ely and Ellijay, Fabius and Flat Rock and Fruitdale, Goshen and Gumboro and Gypsum, Hahira and Happy Jack, Hayden and Hyden and Heber Springs, Ida and Ider and Ila, Jasper and Joplin and Joppa and Juno, Kalamazoo and Kikotsmovi, Kempton and Kirklin and Kokomo, Ladoga and Lamong, Loogootee and Lowpoint, Lim Rock and Rimrock and Paint Rock

Horace P.
McGillicuddy

Smithville
California

and Stony Lonesome, Mayo and Magnolia and McCook, Moodus and Modesto, Nemo and Neodesha and Neshoba, Nameless and Niobrara and Novi, Oiltrough and Oolitic and Ooltewah, Pailo and Paoli, Peoga and Pippa Passes, Plains and Pocahontas, Quaker Hill and Qulin, Raisin, Red Lion, Rifle, and Rocky Face, Shungopovi and Sunbright, Suncook and Sunman, Temperance and Terhune and Truth-or-Consequences, Ulen and Ulm, Umatilla and Utica, Viburnum, Vida, Vidalia, and Viper, War and Wartrace, Winnemucca and Winnetka and Winnipesaukee, Xenia and Xenophon, Yadkin Valley and Yarbro, Yolo and Yuma, Zap and Zebulon, Zion and Zelienople.

Harmonious and poetic, indeed! Yes, from **A** to **Z** and pretty much everywhere in between, it seems our friend Horace has been there – although not necessarily in alphabetical order, of course. Those aren't made-up names; all of those towns are on the maps, you can look them up. Even when he was on the road, Horace knew that for every town he saw, he missed a dozen or a hundred others. Now,

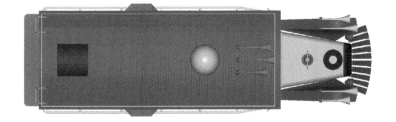

it seems, Horace is catching up. Or the towns are catching up. *Someone* is catching up, anyway.

On and on and on and on the list of towns and cities goes, and it grows, indicating a somewhat logical if disjointed itinerary for a slow but strange – magical? mystical? mythical? – vehicle. The smaller the dots and the print on the maps, and the fainter the lines marking the old local roads, and the more crooked and out-of-the-way those little old roads are, the more likely it seems *The Horace P. McGillicuddy* has been or soon will be spotted.

Yes, that vehicle, that contraption, that marvelous *thing*, that one-man's-masterpiece, whatever it was, whatever it is, and whatever it may seem to be the next time someone sees it, it may still be out there. Still going. Even now. Right now. A little bit behind you, or not too far ahead of you.

Why, early one morning just last week, the folks over in the next county east of us awoke to the eerie sound and the unexpected sight of a strange and wonderful old vehicle that they say was . . . .

**Larry Cloud** is a native of Westfield, Indiana. He has B.S. (1965) and M.S. (1966) degrees in mechanical engineering from Purdue University. He taught mathematics, astronomy, and geology at Tennessee Temple College from 1967 through 1979. Since then he has done a variety of work as an independent machine design engineer.

He continues to live and work, play and worship, and sit and think in Chattanooga, Tennessee.

Made in the USA
Columbia, SC
10 August 2024

39796046R00052